DORR TOWNSHIP LIBRARY (DOR)

0 1341 00075 5117

23.95

DATE DUE

FEB 2 0 2013	
APR 0 8 2014	
WITHDRAWN	

DEMCO, INC. 38-2931

D1256237

Native American Library

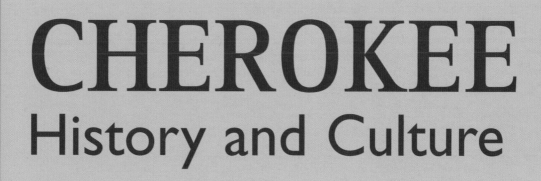

CHEROKEE
History and Culture

Helen Dwyer and D. L. Birchfield

Consultant Robert J. Conley
Sequoyah Distinguished Professor at Western Carolina University

Gareth Stevens
Publishing

Dorr Township Library

Please visit our website, www.garethstevens.com. For a free color catalog of all our high-quality books, call toll free 1-800-542-2595 or fax 1-877-542-2596.

Library of Congress Cataloging-in-Publication Data

Birchfield, D. L., 1948-
Cherokee history and culture / D.L. Birchfield.
    p. cm. — (Native American library)
Includes bibliographical references and index.
ISBN 978-1-4339-5960-8 (pbk.)
ISBN 978-1-4339-5961-5 (6-pack)
ISBN 978-1-4339-5958-5 (library binding)
1. Cherokee Indians—History—Juvenile literature. 2. Cherokee Indians—Social life and customs—Juvenile literature. I. Birchfield, D. L., 1948- Cherokee. II. Title.
E99.C5B482 2011
975.004'97557—dc22

2010052210

New edition published in 2012 by
Gareth Stevens Publishing
111 East 14th Street, Suite 349
New York, NY 10003

First edition published 2005 by Gareth Stevens Publishing

Copyright © 2012 Gareth Stevens Publishing

Produced by Discovery Books
Project editor: Helen Dwyer
Designer and page production: Sabine Beaupré
Photo researchers: Tom Humphrey and Helen Dwyer
Maps: Stefan Chabluk

Photo credits: Cover Stan Honda/Getty Images; Cardaf: p.5; Corbis: pp. 19, 24, 28, 31, 37; FEMA/Bill Koplitz: p. 39; Kaldari: p. 38; Murv Jacob: p. 32 (all); Native Stock: pp. 11, 14 (top), 18 (top), 20, 21, 22, 23 (both), 25 (both), 29, 33, 34, 36; North Wind Picture Archives: pp. 12, 14 (bottom); Peter Newark's American Pictures: pp. 13, 15, 16, 17, 18 (bottom), 30; Shutterstock: pp. 26 (Kirsanov), 27 (Durden Images); ...trials and errors: p. 7; Wolfgang Sauber: p. 9

All rights reserved. No part of this book may be reproduced in any form without permission in writing from the publisher, except by a reviewer.

Printed in the United States of America

CPSIA compliance information: Batch #CS11GS: For further information contact Gareth Stevens, New York, New York at 1-800-542-2595.

CONTENTS

Introduction 4

Chapter 1: Land and Origins. 10

Chapter 2: History 12

Chapter 3: Traditional Way of Life 20

Chapter 4: Cherokee Life Today 30

Chapter 5: A Living Culture 38

Timeline 40

Glossary. 42

More Resources. 44

Things to Think About and Do 46

Index 47

Words that appear in the glossary are printed in **boldface** type the first time they appear in the text.

INTRODUCTION

THE CHEROKEES IN NATIVE AMERICAN HISTORY

The Cherokees are a people originally from the southern Appalachian Mountains. They are just one of the many groups of Native Americans who live today in North America. There are well over five hundred Native American tribes in the United States and more than six hundred in Canada. At least three million people in North America consider themselves to be Native Americans. But who are Native Americans, and how do the Cherokees fit into the history of North America's native peoples?

THE FIRST IMMIGRANTS

Native Americans are people whose **ancestors** settled in North America thousands of years ago. These ancestors probably came from eastern parts of Asia. Their **migrations** probably occurred during cold periods called **ice ages**. At these times, sea levels were much lower than they are now. The area between northeastern Asia and Alaska was dry land, so it was possible to walk between the continents.

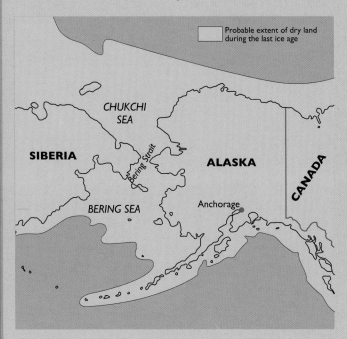

Siberia (Asia) and Alaska (North America) are today separated by an area of ocean named the Bering Strait. During the last ice age, the green area on this map was at times dry land. The Asian ancestors of the Cherokee walked from one continent to the other.

The Cliff Palace at Mesa Verde, Colorado, is the most spectacular example of Native American culture that survives today. It consists of more than 150 rooms and pits built around A.D. 1200 from sandstone blocks.

Scientists are not sure when these migrations took place, but it must have been more than twelve thousand years ago. Around that time, water levels rose and covered the land between Asia and the Americas.

By around ten thousand years ago, the climate had warmed and was similar to conditions today. The first peoples in North America moved around the continent in small groups, hunting wild animals and collecting a wide variety of plant foods. Gradually these groups spread out and lost contact with each other. They developed separate cultures and adopted lifestyles that suited their **environments.**

SETTLING DOWN

Although many tribes continued to gather food and hunt or fish, some Native Americans began to live in settlements and grow crops. Their homes ranged from underground pit houses and huts of mud and thatch to dwellings in cliffs. By 3500 B.C., a plentiful supply of fish in the Pacific Ocean and in rivers had enabled people to settle in large coastal villages from Alaska to Washington State. In the deserts of Arizona more than two thousand years later, farmers constructed hundreds of miles of **irrigation** canals to carry water to their crops.

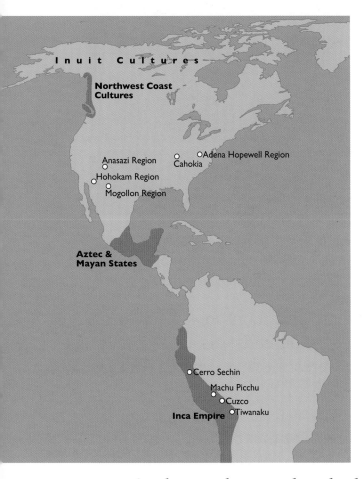

Inuit Cultures

Northwest Coast
Cultures

Anasazi Region
Hohokam Region
Mogollon Region

Cahokia
Adena Hopewell Region

Aztec &
Mayan States

Cerro Sechin
Machu Picchu
Cuzco
Tiwanaku
Inca Empire

This map highlights some of the main Native American cultures that flourished at various times before Europeans arrived in the Americas.

In the Ohio River valley between 700 B.C. and A.D. 500, people of the Adena and Hopewell **cultures** built clusters of large burial mounds, such as the Serpent Mound in Ohio, which survives today. In the Mississippi **floodplains**, the Native peoples formed complex societies. They created mud and thatch temples on top of flat earth pyramids. Their largest town, Cahokia, in Illinois, contained more than one hundred mounds and may have been home to thirty thousand people.

By around A.D. 1500, the Cherokees created large towns and villages in the Appalachian Mountains. They grew a variety of crops in the valleys, gathered wild plant food, hunted, and fished.

CONTACT WITH EUROPEANS

Around A.D. 1500, European ships reached North America. The first explorers were the Spanish. Armed with guns and riding horses, they took over land and forced the Native Americans to work for them. The Spanish were followed by the British, Dutch, and French, who were looking for land to settle and for opportunities to trade. In the later 1600s, the Cherokees began to trade with English settlers. Some of these settlers took over Cherokee land.

When Native Americans met these Europeans they came into contact with diseases, such as smallpox and measles, that they had never experienced before. At least one half of all Native Americans, and possibly many more than that, were unable to overcome these diseases and died.

Guns were also disastrous for Native Americans. At first, only the Europeans had guns, which enabled them to overcome native peoples in fights and battles. Eventually, Native Americans groups obtained guns and used them in conflicts with each other. Native American groups were also forced to take sides and fight in wars between the French and British.

Horses, too, had a big influence in Native American lifestyles, especially on the Great Plains. Some groups became horse breeders and traders. People were able to travel greater distances and began to hunt buffalo on horseback. Soon horses became central to Plains trade and social life.

At the end of the 1700s, people of European descent began to migrate over the Appalachian Mountains, looking for new land to farm and exploit. By the middle of the nineteenth century, they had reached the west coast of North America. This expansion was disastrous for Native Americans.

Sequoyah invented the Cherokee syllabary, or writing system, in 1821. It uses a different symbol for each syllable and is still used by modern Cherokees.

RESERVATION LIFE

Many peoples were pressured into moving onto **reservations** in the west. The biggest of these reservations later became the U.S. state of Oklahoma. Native Americans who tried to remain in their homelands were attacked and defeated.

In the winter of 1838–1839, the U.S. Army forced the Cherokees to walk from their homelands to present-day Oklahoma. Thousands died on the journey. Only a few Cherokees in North Carolina were allowed to remain in their homeland.

New laws in the United States and Canada took away most of the control Native Americans had over their lives. They were expected to give up their cultures and adopt the ways and habits of white Americans. It became a crime to practice their traditional religions. Children were taken from their homes and placed in boarding schools, where they were forbidden to speak their native languages.

Despite this **persecution**, many Native Americans clung on to their cultures through the first half of the twentieth century. The Society of American Indians was founded in 1911 and its campaign for U.S. citizenship for Native Americans was successful in 1924. Other Native American

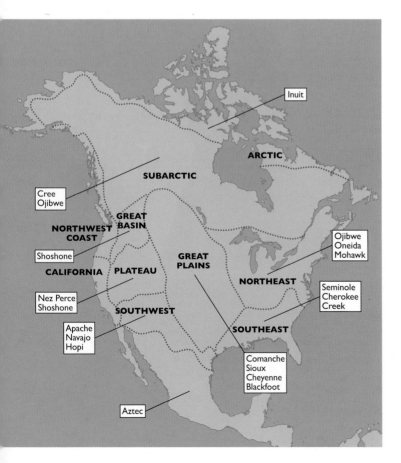

Cree
Ojibwe

NORTHWEST COAST

GREAT BASIN

Shoshone

CALIFORNIA PLATEAU

Nez Perce
Shoshone

SOUTHWEST

Apache
Navajo
Hopi

Aztec

Inuit

ARCTIC

SUBARCTIC

GREAT PLAINS

NORTHEAST

Ojibwe
Oneida
Mohawk

Seminole
Cherokee
Creek

SOUTHEAST

Comanche
Sioux
Cheyenne
Blackfoot

This map of North America highlights the main Native American cultural groups, along with the smaller groups, or tribes, featured in this series of books.

The Cherokee Heritage Center in Tahlequah, Oklahoma, includes a reconstruction of a seventeeth century Cherokee village, as it would have been before European contact.

organizations were formed to promote traditional cultures and to campaign politically for Native American rights.

THE ROAD TO SELF-GOVERNMENT

Despite these campaigns, Native Americans on reservations endured poverty and very low standards of living. Many of them moved away to work and live in cities, where they hoped life would be better. In most cases, they found life just as difficult. They not only faced **discrimination** and **prejudice** but also could not compete successfully for jobs against more established ethnic groups.

In the 1970s, the American Indian Movement (AIM) organized large protests that attracted attention worldwide. They highlighted the problems of unemployment, discrimination, and poverty that Native Americans experienced in North America.

The AIM protests led to changes in policy. Some new laws protected the civil rights of Native Americans, while other laws allowed tribal governments to be formed. Today tribal governments have a wide range of powers. They operate large businesses and run their own schools and health care.

Chapter 1

LAND AND ORIGINS

CHEROKEE COUNTRY

The Cherokees are a North American Native people whose home-lands in the southern Appalachian Mountains once included parts of present-day Kentucky, West Virginia, Virginia, North Carolina, South Carolina, Georgia, Alabama, and Tennessee. They are by far the largest Native **nation** in the United States, with a total tribal membership close to 275,000 people. Many Cherokees are mixed bloods — part Indian, part non-Indian — due to their long history of **intermarriage** with whites.

Today, about ten thousand Eastern Cherokees live on or near the Qualla Boundary reservation in North Carolina, but most Cherokees live in the Cherokee Nation in northeastern Oklahoma. Many thousands also live throughout the United States and in Canada.

The Cherokees' homeland once included a large area of today's southeastern United States. Most Cherokee villages were in the southern Appalachian Mountains of present-day North Carolina, Georgia, and Tennessee.

CHEROKEE ORIGINS

No one knows for sure how long Cherokees and other Indians might have been in North America, how they got here, or from where they came. Cherokee origin stories tell of a time when

Home of Cherokees for centuries, the southern Appalachian Mountains in North Carolina are a place of great natural beauty. Today, the Great Smoky Mountains National Park is located near the reservation of the Eastern Band Cherokee Indians.

water covered the earth. Land was formed when a water beetle dove deep into the ocean and scooped up mud, bringing it to the surface to make the earth.

The name *Cherokee* (or *Tsa-la-gi*) is thought to be a Choctaw word meaning "cave people." The Cherokees' name for themselves is *Ani-yun-wiya,* meaning the "real people" or "original people."

Cherokee Words

Cherokee is an **Iroquoian** language that is distantly related to the language of the Mohawks and other Iroquoian tribes in the Northeast. Some scholars estimate that it has been developing separately for about thirty-five hundred years.

Cherokee	Pronunciation	English
asgaya	ahs-kay-ya	man
agehya	ah-gay-hyuh	woman
sogwili	so-gwee-lee	horse
osiyo	oh-see-yo	hello
awi	ah-whee	deer
saloli	sa-lo-li	squirrel
galijodii	gahl-jo-dee	house

HISTORY

Chapter 2

THE EUROPEANS ARRIVE

Before Europeans came to North America, Cherokees were farmers living in villages in Appalachian Mountain valleys. They harvested large crops of corn, beans, and squash and gathered nuts, berries, wild onions, and other food in the forest. Hunting provided meat.

By the early 1600s, the English had established colonies along the Atlantic coast. Settlers soon began taking over Cherokee land in Virginia, forcing some villages to relocate farther inland in the Appalachian Mountains, where most Cherokees lived. By the 1670s, Cherokees were trading with the English, exchanging deerskins and animal furs for metal pots, knives, axes, and other useful things. Before long, they began trading for guns, which they soon became dependent upon.

POWER PROVIDES LITTLE PROTECTION

By 1729, about twenty thousand Cherokees lived in about sixty-four towns. Though a powerful nation, the Cherokees were not able to avoid the wars that Europeans fought with

Made in the 1660s, this painting shows the Indian village of Secotan in North Carolina. At that time, North Carolina was part of Virginia Colony.

one another in North America, and European armies sometimes burned Indian villages during their own battles.

This portrait was drawn of three Cherokee chiefs in 1762, when they were visiting London, England.

As the United States became independent from England in 1783, the country's desire for land — even that belonging to the Cherokees — grew. Settlers flocked into Cherokee country, including present-day Georgia. When the new nation acquired land west of the Mississippi River in the Louisiana Purchase in 1803, President Thomas Jefferson decided that all the eastern Indian nations would have to give up their own land and move west. The federal government would remove the Indians; Georgia's government agreed.

President Jefferson's Indian Policy

President Thomas Jefferson played a big role in the Cherokees losing their land. In 1803, Jefferson began a scheme to give the Indians unlimited **credit** at government-owned trading posts, hoping they would go deeply into debt buying trade goods. They would then have to trade their land to the government to pay their bills. That's exactly what happened; each U.S. **treaty** with the Cherokees required them to give up more land. Thus, the United States acquired millions of acres of land very cheaply.

The first Native American-language newspaper, the *Cherokee Phoenix*, in 1828. It used the set of written Cherokee characters invented by Sequoyah.

A Time of Change

The Cherokees realized they could lose their ancient homeland and tried to avoid removal by embracing many white practices, hoping the whites would then consider them as equals. They adopted a written **constitution** and laws, forming a government modeled on that of the United States. They changed the way they dressed and began looking like the white settlers.

They also invited **missionaries** into their nation, who started schools and churches.

Once Sequoyah had invented a way of writing the Cherokee language that could be learned quickly and easily, the Cherokees soon learned how to use it. They began publishing their own newspaper, the *Cherokee Phoenix,* in both English and Cherokee.

This painting shows gold miners in the Cherokee country in present-day Georgia in the late 1820s. The "Southern Gold Rush" on Cherokee land caused many Americans, especially Georgians, to demand Cherokee removal.

LAND IN DANGER

Nothing the Cherokees did, however, satisfied the people of Georgia, who wanted Indian land. In 1828, General Andrew Jackson was elected president, promising to remove the Indians from the South. In 1829, gold was discovered in the southern part of the Cherokee Nation, and a wild gold rush started. Miners stole the Cherokee gold and demanded the Indians give up their land.

In 1830, Congress passed the Indian Removal Act. The Cherokees also began to use the legal system to protect their rights, however, winning an important decision from the U.S. Supreme Court. This 1832 case made clear that Georgia could not extend its laws into the Cherokee Nation and that the tribe was an independent nation. The Cherokees gained the respect and sympathy of many Americans, who protested Georgia's demand that the Natives move.

In 1835, ignoring the 1832 Supreme Court decision, President Jackson pressured a small **minority** of Cherokees — who were not elected by their people — into signing a removal treaty. These Cherokees quickly moved to the West, but the great majority of the tribe, under Chief John Ross, refused to leave. They clung to the hope that they would not be forced to forsake their ancient homeland.

Son of a Scottish father and an Indian mother, Chief John Ross led his people on the forced march to Indian Territory from 1838 to 1839.

It is no doubt good policy in the states to get rid of all the Indians within their limits as soon as possible; [but] in doing so, they care very little where they send them, provided they get them out of the limits of their state. . . . This we consider the worst policy our government can pursue with the Indians.

Arkansas Gazette, *1829, Arkansas Territory*

U.S. Army General Winfield Scott was in charge of the Cherokee removal. He became a war hero during the Mexican-American War of 1846 to 1848.

Men working in the fields were arrested and driven to the **stockades**. Women were dragged from their homes by soldiers whose language they could not understand. Children were often separated from their parents and driven into the stockades. . . . And often the old and the infirm were prodded with bayonets to hasten them to the stockade.

U.S. Army Private John G. Burnett, who participated in the Cherokee removal of 1838

THE TRAIL OF TEARS

Cherokee removal came suddenly. In 1838, General Winfield Scott invaded the Cherokee country with seven thousand U.S. Army soldiers and Georgia volunteers. They swept through the countryside, rounding up Cherokee families by the thousands and herding them into prison camps. Hundreds of Cherokees died there from disease.

During the winter of 1838 to 1839, the U.S. Army divided the Cherokees into thirteen groups of about one thousand each and started them west. Many had to walk barefoot on the frozen ground, without enough food and with only one blanket per person for shelter from the cold. The Cherokees traveled about 800 miles (1,300 kilometers) to present-day northeastern Oklahoma, leaving their dead along the way. Their terrible journey became known as the Trail of Tears.

The removal killed about four thousand Cherokees, but many more died of illness after arriving in the West. The Cherokee removal was one of the cruelest episodes in U.S. history.

LEFT BEHIND

When the great majority of Cherokees were removed in the 1830s, several hundred tribal members in North Carolina claimed they lived outside the Cherokee

No one painted the Cherokee removal of 1838 to 1839 at the time, but this later painting, by Robert Lindneux, is his interpretation of what the removal might have looked like.

Nation on land **ceded** to the United States in earlier treaties. Though their legal status was greatly in doubt, the U.S. Army did not attempt to remove them.

LIFE IN THE NEW LAND

Forced to leave their homeland, some Cherokees turned on the small minority of Cherokees who had signed the treaty. In 1839, some of those signers were killed, and the nation was thrown into unrest.

It was seven years before the Cherokees living in the West finally made an uneasy peace among themselves and began rebuilding their lives. Under Chief John Ross,

I fought through the civil war and have seen men shot to pieces and slaughtered by thousands, but the Cherokee removal was the cruelest work I ever knew.

A Confederate Civil War colonel, who had participated in the Cherokee removal in 1838 as a Georgia volunteer

This painting, by John Mix Stanley, depicts a gathering of seventeen Indian nations in 1843 in Tahlequah in the Cherokee Nation. The Cherokees sponsored this meeting to discuss common problems.

DҺGWУ

JOᏰᏬVᎫ JᎥᏚᏩᎢᎳᎫ.

CHEROKEE PRIMER.

- PARK HILL:
Mission Press. John Candy, Printer.
DᎾ ᎤҺᏴᎡᎫᏍ: ᏓᏲᏛᏆᏓ, JᏚᏴᏔᎾ-Ꭿ.
::::::::
1845.

The Cherokee Primer, 1845. This small book was used by children in the Cherokee Nation public school system. By the late nineteenth century, the Cherokees had developed a school system that was better than that of most states in the region.

they created a Cherokee public school system and two colleges, called seminaries. They published the *Cherokee Advocate* newspaper and governed themselves under a written constitution, modeled somewhat on the U.S. Constitution, with officials elected in general elections.

CIVIL WAR ERUPTS

The U.S. government had promised in treaties to protect the Cherokees, but when the **Civil War** broke out in 1861, the government withdrew all its troops in their lands, leaving the Indians helpless. Many had to flee from their homes as armies from both sides swept through their land, stealing all their food and animals and burning almost all the buildings. About one-fourth of the Cherokee people died during the war, mostly from starvation and disease in **refugee** camps.

Cherokees fought on both sides during the war, but the victorious North treated

The U.S. Congress began forcing the Cherokees to give up their land in the late nineteenth century. The Cherokee Strip was opened up to whites in a land run in 1893; they raced one another to stake a claim to a farm.

all Cherokees as defeated enemies at the war's end, forcing them to sign a harsh treaty in 1866. The treaty required them to give up land, allow the railroad to build in their nation, and put them under U.S. laws. After the war, whites swarmed onto the Cherokee Nation until they outnumbered the Indians and began demanding their land.

DIVIDING THE LAND AND PEOPLE

During the 1890s, Congress forced the Cherokees to divide the land held by the tribe as a whole and accept individual ownership of small farms; the government then sold the remaining Cherokee land to white settlers. In 1907, when the state of Oklahoma was created, the U.S. government claimed that the Cherokee Nation had been abolished.

For most of the twentieth century, the U.S. government tried to end the status of the Cherokees and other Indian groups as independent nations. Until the 1970s, in fact, Cherokee chiefs were appointed by the U.S. president, sometimes only for one day, just to have someone to sign legal papers.

A Promise Broken
The United States hereby . . . agree that the lands ceded to the Cherokee nation . . . [will never] be included within the territorial limits . . . of any State or Territory.

U.S. government's treaty with the Cherokees, 1835

Chapter 3

TRADITIONAL WAY OF LIFE

A FARMING PEOPLE

The traditional Cherokee lifestyle was based on farming; hunting and fishing also provided food. Everyone helped with the town farm plots, and the resulting crops belonged to all. Each family also worked its own fields. Those farms, as well as the family houses, belonged to the women.

The Cherokees were expert farmers, growing mainly corn, beans, and squash, as well as many other crops, such as melons and tobacco. They also raised turkeys for food as well as hunting them in the wild. After Europeans introduced hogs, cattle, chickens, and horses, Cherokees soon reared these in large numbers, too.

Traditional Cherokee food is an important part of many Cherokee gatherings. Here, the feast includes pig back fat, mustard greens, chestnut bread, and butternut squash.

A Land of Plenty

Experts at harvesting the natural resources of their homeland, Cherokees gathered large crops of pecans and other nuts in the fall, wild onions in the spring, and the blackberries that grew thickly on the hillsides in the summer. Deer, elk, bears, mountain lions, and wolves filled their forests, while herds of buffalo grazed on the famous "blue grass" prairies of their hunting grounds.

European trade goods brought great changes. To have deer hides and animal furs to trade, the Cherokee had to hunt the animals as they never had before — for money. Soon their prey became scarce; the hunters

Finely crafted Cherokee pottery was an important part of their trade goods as well as their home life.

couldn't gather enough hides and furs for trade. Before long, the Cherokees had little to trade except their land.

"Five Civilized Tribes"

European settlers called the Cherokees, along with the Choctaws, Chickasaws, Seminoles, and Muskogee/Creeks, the Five Civilized Tribes. The settlers were impressed when they saw these skilled farmers who lived mostly in their own large towns in highly organized societies. The Cherokees were also gifted public speakers and diplomats, quickly earning the respect of the Europeans who settled near them.

In a historical Cherokee village, built for tourists, visitors can see how a traditional Cherokee house was constructed.

CHEROKEE TOWNS

Cherokee villages were often built like forts, with a high stockade fence made of logs surrounding them. In the center of the village stood at least one large building for public meetings, other public buildings for storing corn, and ball fields for playing games. Cherokee homes, with walls of branches held together with mud, surrounded the central public area.

Each town had its own independent government. All the men and women were allowed to speak when discussing issues. Decisions were not by majority vote, but by **consensus**, meaning that most people finally reached agreement. Cherokees who did not agree with the consensus were free to ignore the decision, move to another village, or start a new village of their own.

FAMILY LIFE

Children spent most of their time playing, often with a blowgun made by an older relative from a long piece of cane. Spending many hours hunting squirrels and rabbits in the woods near the village, they learned to shoot darts through the blowgun. When the children were older, they received a bow and arrows and learned to hunt larger game, such as deer. By the time they were teenagers, most young Cherokees were expert hunters.

Generally, women took care of the home, cooked, made clothing, and tended the agricultural fields, while men hunted, made weapons, and fought enemies in times of war. Women could also become warriors, however. Most women did not choose to do so, but some who did became famous, earning the respected name "War Woman."

In a reconstructed Cherokee village at the Cherokee Heritage Center in the Cherokee Nation near Tahlequah, a woman is showing how to grind corn into cornmeal.

Cherokee Clothing

Before European contact, traditional Cherokee summer clothing consisted of a **breechcloth** and **moccasins** for most men and a short skirt for women. In cold weather, women added a pull-over top, and men wore a hunting jacket and leggings. All were made of deerskin.

During the 1800s, men began wearing shirts and jackets made of cloth, and women began weaving blouses and long dresses. Some men also wore a turban around their head. By the late 1800s, many Cherokees dressed like the white people on the frontier.

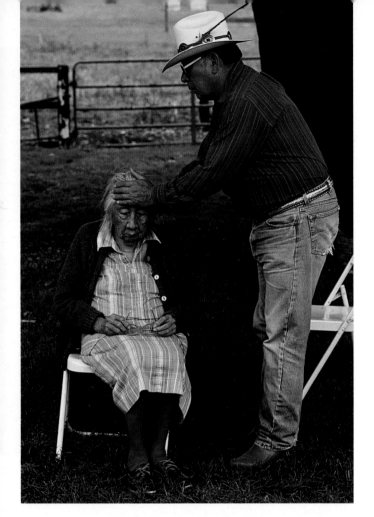

A woman visits a Cherokee **medicine man**. Today, many Cherokees still prefer to seek the knowledge that traditional doctors have learned from many centuries of traditional Cherokee medical practice.

TRADITIONAL STORIES

Stories are an important part of Cherokee traditional life, teaching children about their history, traditions, culture, and the morals of the Cherokee belief system. For example, traditional stories explain the origin of illness and its treatment. According to one such traditional story, long ago, the animals held a council to discuss a problem: the people were killing too many animals without showing proper respect for the lives they were taking. Each animal created an illness that would punish the people.

When the plants heard what the animals were doing, they felt sorry for the people, and each plant created a cure for an illness. The story explains how the Cherokees had to learn to show respect for the lives of animals they took and to live in harmony with the animals and plants.

TRADITIONAL GAMES

Games have also formed a vital part of Cherokee traditional life. Stickball games, similar to the game of lacrosse, between Cherokee towns were by far the most important. All other

Cherokee women playing stickball. The game is an ancient part of Cherokee culture, and it remains important to all the southeastern Indian tribes and to many other tribes in North America.

activities came to a standstill when a stickball match was being played. Medicine men for both sides were employed to make charms that might bring victory in the game. Frequently, the people of the opposing towns bet everything of any value that they possessed on the outcome of the game. Today, stickball is often played both as a game and as an important part of rituals at ceremonial grounds.

Stickball sticks were made of hickory, with a webbed pocket made of leather. The ball was originally made of deerskin.

Stickball Games

The favorite time is in the fall, after the corn has ripened . . . at this season a game takes place somewhere on the reservation at least every other week . . . but the exact spot selected [for the game] is always a matter of uncertainty up to the last moment. . . . If this were not the case, a spy from the other settlement might [try] to insure the defeat of the party by strewing along their trail a soup made of the hamstrings of rabbits, which would have the effect of rendering the players [timid] and easily confused.

James Mooney, a scholar and author, in 1890

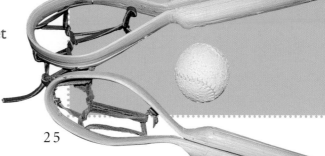

The Animals' Ball Game

Many Cherokee **myths** explain how different species of animals acquired their striking physical features. The following story tells how flying mammals were created.

One day, the four-legged animals challenged the birds to a ball game. The birds accepted the challenge but they feared they could not compete against the bear's strength and the deer's speed. While they were discussing their tactics, two small four-legged animals appeared. They said that the bigger animals had refused to let them play in the animal team and they asked to join the birds' team.

The birds felt sorry for the little animals and decided to let them play, but first they had to be able to fly. So the birds found a drum covered in groundhog skin. They cut the skin into two pieces and attached it to two sticks. These artificial wings were then fastened to one of the small mammals. And so the first bat was created.

There was no more skin left to make another pair of wings, so two large birds took hold of the fur on either side of the other

To find their way around, bats constantly emit sounds and gather information about the objects around them from the echoes. They do this so well they can weave in and out of trees in a forest at night. The Cherokees noticed this dodging behavior and described it in their story.

The Cherokee story says that after the ball game, the martin was rewarded with a gourd because he caught the ball and that this is the reason that martins nest in gourds.

small mammal's body. Then they pulled until the skin between his front and back legs became stretched. And so the first flying squirrel was created.

When the teams were ready, the game began. The flying squirrel caught the ball and carried it to a tree. It threw the ball to the birds, who passed it around in the air, out of reach of the animals. But then they made a mistake and dropped the ball. It fell toward the bear, but just in time the martin swooped past and scooped it up just above the ground. The martin passed the ball to the bat, who dodged and circled around the animals and finally scored. Thanks mainly to their two new friends, the birds had won the game, and the animals had never touched the ball.

BELIEFS

In Cherokee traditional culture, the world was described as being like a giant bowl turned upside down on a saucer, forming a big dome. The earth is underneath the dome, floating on water. The sky fills the dome all the way to the underside of the bowl, which is called the Sky Vault. The Sun travels across the sky each day just beneath the Sky Vault, which is made of rock. At the end of its journey, it slips underneath the Sky Vault so it can return to its starting point and cross the sky again the next day.

This mask is used for a traditional Cherokee dance called the Booger Dance. Dances have always been important community activities for Cherokees, a time of feasting and visiting.

On top of the Sky Vault is another world, very much like the earth. The souls of departed Cherokees live there, along with spirit beings.

Another world also exists underneath the earth, but it is just the opposite of life on the earth. When it is daytime on the earth, it is nighttime there. When it is summer on the earth, it is winter there. This underworld is home for many powerful, dangerous spirit forces.

The worlds above and below the earth represent extremes. Traditional Cherokees believe that they live their lives between those two extremes, constantly trying to maintain harmony and balance between the two. Most Cherokee rituals, ceremonies, and the old habits of living are intended to help maintain that balance and harmony.

Stomp Dance

The Cherokee Stomp Dance is a sacred dance, ordinarily held at Stomp Grounds in the countryside. Each of the Grounds has its own religious leaders. Their locations are unknown to non-Cherokees; they are not for tourists. The dance is performed in a counterclockwise direction around a sacred fire. Participants engage in this and other dances and ceremonies all night long, once a month between spring and fall. Occasionally, the Stomp Dance is also performed at other cultural events as a way of teaching others about traditional Cherokee life.

Children being taught the Cherokee Stomp Dance. These dances are very popular today. Some are held in public; others take place at more remote Stomp Grounds in the countryside.

CHEROKEE LIFE TODAY

Chapter 4

LITERATURE AND ART

The Cherokees have produced many scholars, writers, **playwrights**, poets, actors, and artists. Some world-famous people, such as Oklahoma humorist Will Rogers, had Cherokee blood.

Lynn Riggs (1899–1954) wrote stories, poems, and 21 plays. One of his plays, called *Green Grow the Lilacs*, was later converted into a musical by Richard Rodgers and Oscar Hammerstein. This became one of the most famous Broadway plays of all time — *Oklahoma!*

Poet Geary Hobson, author of *Deer Hunting and Other Poems,* is a professor of English at the University of Oklahoma. He edited one of the most important collections of American Indian literature, *The Remembered Earth,* which was published in 1981.

Rennard Strickland has become one of the foremost scholars on Indian law. He was president of the American Association of Law Schools in 1994.

A number of Cherokees are currently working with materials

Entertainer and humorist Will Rogers (1879–1935) became one of the best-known Cherokees in the world. He is shown here at his first vaudeville appearance in New York City in 1905.

from their traditional culture. Martha Berry has researched historical beadwork and creates beadwork bags, moccasins, belts, sashes, and purses in styles that were popular more than 150 years ago. Some of her designs illustrate Cherokee stories.

An acclaimed author of children's books about Cherokee life, storyteller Gail Ross has entertained thousands of people with traditional tales. Novelist Robert J. Conley brings alive the oldest Cherokee stories about their history in his Real People series. He has received the Cherokee Medal of Honor from the Cherokee Honor Society and is now in the Oklahoma Professional Writers Hall of Fame. Conley is author of more than eighty books and is currently the Sequoyah Distinguished Professor at Western Carolina University and President of Western Writers of America.

An international opera star, Barbara McAlister sometimes sings an ancient lullaby, one of the oldest surviving Cherokee songs, in her performances.

Wes Studi

Famous for his Hollywood movies, Oklahoma Cherokee actor Wes Studi starred in *Geronimo: An American Legend*. He also played the role of Magua in *Last of the Mohicans* and a Powhatan chief in *The New World*. In 2009, he appeared in the miniseries *We Shall Remain* and spoke the Cherokee language throughout. Studi began his career with the American Indian Theatre Company in Tulsa, Oklahoma, as actor and playwright, and he keeps in close contact with his people.

Cherokee actor Wes Studi, as he appeared in the movie *Geronimo: An American Legend*. Wes Studi has become one of the busiest and best-known Native American actors in Hollywood.

Grandmother Stories

Artist Murv Jacob paints pictures of traditional life. He and author Deborah L. Duvall have together produced two series of books called Grandmother Stories and Cherokee World Stories. Each book retells a Cherokee animal legend in up-to-date language and is illustrated with black-ink or color pictures on every page. Jacob and Duvall have also created several e-books of stories, which can be seen and read online.

Murv Jacob with the Grandmother Stories he illustrated.

Two of Murv Jacob's color illustrations of Cherokee tales.

Like children everywhere, Cherokee schoolchildren love recess. This school is located on the Qualla Boundary reservation in North Carolina.

THE EASTERN CHEROKEES

In the mid-nineteenth century, William Thomas, a white man raised by Eastern Cherokees, bought land for them at the edge of the mountains, property that later became known as the Qualla Boundary. After the Civil War, others joined the Eastern Cherokees on their reservation in North Carolina.

During the twentieth century, tourism became the most important part of the Eastern Cherokees' **economy**, especially after 1940 when the Great Smoky Mountains National Park opened next to the reservation. Today, they have added a **casino** to their economy, and millions of tourists visit the reservation each year. Parts of the casino profits are used to protect the environment, preserve Cherokee **heritage**, and improve health care, education, and housing.

By the early twenty-first century, the Eastern Band owned more than 56,000 acres (22,700 hectares) of land. Their population is now more than ten thousand. Eastern Cherokees have little opportunity for continuing their centuries-old skills as farmers except for raising family vegetable gardens. Most of their reservation is now mountain land thickly covered with trees.

THE WESTERN CHEROKEES

Today, two Cherokee tribes now lie within the boundaries of the Cherokee Nation in the West — the United Keetoowah Band of Cherokee Indians, Oklahoma, and the Cherokee Nation. Numbering ten thousand members, the Keetoowah Band is much smaller than the Cherokee Nation.

Both the Keetoowah Band and the Cherokee Nation have their tribal headquarters in Tahlequah, Oklahoma, the historic capitol

Cherokee women compete in a blowgun contest. With practice, the blowgun can be used with great accuracy.

of the Cherokees in the West. The Cherokee Nation, with over 240,000, is not only the largest Cherokee tribe but also the largest Indian nation in the United States by far. It was reorganized in the 1970s. The Cherokee Nation gained federal recognition under a new constitution when the U.S. government gave up its 1907 claim that Indian tribes in Oklahoma had been abolished when that territory became a state.

The Cherokee Nation today includes the same land as the old Cherokee Nation did in Indian Territory. The Cherokee Nation and the State of Oklahoma both claim the same land.

A NATION RENEWED

As the U.S. government changed its policy toward Native American governments and upheld laws to allow them to govern themselves, the Cherokee Nation became a leader among Indian tribes. It now manages many tribal programs, ranging from educational programs for Cherokee children to housing programs, that were once run by the U.S. government. This has helped make the Cherokee Nation a large employer in the region, a multimillion-dollar enterprise with a great impact on the local economy.

EDUCATION

Today, Cherokee Nation children in northeastern Oklahoma again have an opportunity to learn from Cherokee teachers. Many state public schools in the Nation have Cherokee cultural programs funded by the U.S. government, and many also have Head Start programs, which offer early learning opportunities, for preschoolers. The Cherokee Nation now operates Sequoyah High School, which used to be a boarding school run by the U.S. government, in Tahlequah.

Many young Cherokees stay at home to go to college. Northeastern Oklahoma State University, in Tahlequah, has the highest enrollment of Indian college students of any university in the United States, more than one thousand Indian students each semester. Many of those college students become schoolteachers in the Oklahoma public school system.

The Cherokee Nation headquarters building near Tahlequah. The Cherokee Nation tribal complex has many buildings, including a restaurant and gift shop.

Wilma Mankiller

Wilma Mankiller was born in Tahlequah, Oklahoma, in 1945. The family name is a traditional Cherokee military rank. Her first family home, which she shared with her parents and ten brothers and sisters, was a farmhouse without plumbing or electricity. Later the family moved to San Francisco, where Wilma attended high school and university. She became Native American programs coordinator with Oakland public schools before she returned to Tahlequah in 1976 and became a Cherokee Nation tribal planner. Mankiller gained international recognition as a political leader as the first female principal chief of the Cherokee Nation from 1985 to 1995. During that time, she guided her people into the modern era by helping the Cherokee Nation gain the right to self-government. She also brought needed programs and services to the tribe. In 1998, she received the Congressional Medal of Freedom from President Bill Clinton. A leader among Natives and non-Natives alike, she spoke publicly on issues of concern to Indians and women. After her death in 2010, the Cherokee Nation Tribal Council named Wilma Mankiller a National Treasure of the Cherokee Nation.

Wilma Mankiller and President Reagan (left) in a 1988 meeting at the White House.

Chapter 5

A LIVING CULTURE

A LIVING LANGUAGE

Keeping the Cherokee language alive is a main priority of the tribes today. Most Native speakers are older people, and numbers are falling. Among the Eastern Cherokees only around 300 people still speak the language.

A **bilingual** school sign at the entrance to Cherokee Central Schools in Cherokee, North Carolina.

Since 2000, the Cherokee tribes have attempted to preserve their language by setting up immersion schools. Children in immersion schools are taught, speak, and write only in Cherokee. The Cherokee Nation Immersion School in Tahlequah opened in 2003 as a preschool class. Since then it has expanded to include all classes up to fifth grade and has around one hundred students. In 2009, the Eastern Cherokees opened a similar immersion school, the Kituwah Language Academy, in Cherokee, North Carolina.

CHEROKEE HERITAGE

The Cherokee Heritage Center in Tahlequah and the Museum of the Cherokee Indian in Cherokee, North Carolina, both inform visitors about the history and culture of the Cherokees. In 2010,

The Cherokee National Youth Choir takes part in celebrations in Washington, D.C. The choir was founded in 2000 and performs traditional songs in the Cherokee language. It has already recorded several successful albums. The choir's members are Cherokee middle- and high-school students.

another heritage museum, the Cherokee National Supreme Court Museum, opened in Tahlequah. This historic building, the oldest government building in Oklahoma, focuses on the history of Cherokee law, newspapers, and language.

The Cherokee people, both Eastern and Western, have entered the twenty-first century with renewed hope for the future. They are once again governing themselves and are seeking more self-determination for their futures.

Cherokee and Computers

Since 2003, the written Cherokee language, known as the Cherokee Syllabary, has been gradually incorporated into computer software. First the Cherokee script was turned into a computer font. Then in 2010 it became the first Native American language to be available on Apple iPhones and iPods.

Using the Cherokee Syllabary has become easier since the Cherokee Nation's Cultural Resources department developed a special computer keypad, which fits over the top of an ordinary keypad. It requires fewer keystrokes than previously to type in Cherokee, so users will be able to type faster. The new keypad should benefit all users of the syllabary, from children in Cherokee immersion schools to Cherokee language undergraduates and translators.

Dorr Township Library

TIMELINE

1500s	Cherokees living in villages in Appalachian mountain valleys.
1540	Cherokees encounter Spanish explorers in Georgia and the Carolinas.
1670s	Cherokees already trading with English settlers.
early 1700s	Cherokees living in about 64 towns.
1730s	First Christian missionaries arrive in Cherokee lands.
1738	Smallpox kills more than one quarter of Cherokees.
1776	American Revolution; most Cherokees side with the English.
1785	Cherokees agree to first treaty with the United States.
1803	U.S. government outlaws Indians owning land within Georgia, urges Eastern tribes to move west.
1817	In U.S. treaty, Cherokees trade for some land in West; some Cherokee "old settlers" volunteer to move there.
1821	Sequoyah invents a system of writing the Cherokee language.
1827	The Cherokee Nation adopts constitution; elects John Ross chief.
1828	First Indian language newspaper, *Cherokee Phoenix*, is founded.
1829	Georgians discover gold on Cherokee land; Georgia legislature tries to extend state laws over Cherokees.
1835	Small number of Cherokees sign treaty agreeing to move.
1838–39	General Winfield Scott's large U.S. Army invades Cherokee homeland; Cherokee Trail of Tears; forced removal of 17,000 Cherokees; thousands die.

1840s	Cherokees rebuild their lives in the West, adopt new Cherokee constitution, and establish *Cherokee Advocate*.
1861–65	U.S. Civil War devastates Cherokee land.
1867	Cherokee National Capitol is built in Tahlequah.
1887	Congress passes law to divide tribal lands; remaining land sold to white settlers.
1889	Eastern Cherokee reservation established in North Carolina.
1907	Government claims Cherokee Nation no longer exists.
1900s	U.S. presidents appoint Cherokee chiefs because federal government needs someone to sign legal papers occasionally.
1946	United Keetoowah Band of Cherokee Indians gains federal recognition.
late 1960s	Violent Indian protests focus world attention on treatment of Native Americans in the United States.
early 1970s	U.S. government allows Cherokees to adopt new constitutions and form tribal governments again; W. W. Keeler becomes principal chief of the Cherokee Nation.
1985–1995	Wilma Mankiller is principal chief of the Cherokee Nation.
1990	Cherokees take control of many federal Cherokee programs.
1995	Joe Byrd elected principal chief of the Cherokee Nation.
2000	Chad Smith elected principal chief of the Cherokee Nation.
2000s	Cherokee immersion schools opened in Oklahoma and North Carolina; Cherokee syllabary available on computers.
2010	Cherokee syllabary available on iPhones and iPods.

GLOSSARY

ancestors: people from whom an individual or group is descended.

bilingual: able to speak two languages fluently.

breechcloth: strip of cloth worn around the hips.

casino: a building that has slot machines, card games, and other gambling games.

ceded: gave up ownership of something.

Civil War: the war between northern and southern U.S. states that lasted from 1861 to 1865.

consensus: an agreement among all individuals in a group to an opinion or position.

constitution: the basic laws and principles of a nation that outline the powers of the government and the rights of the people.

credit: the ability to make purchases without paying money for the items immediately.

culture: the arts, beliefs, and customs that form a people's way of life.

discrimination: unjust treatment usually because of a person's race or sex.

economy: the way a country or people produces, divides up, and uses its goods and money.

environment: objects and conditions all around that affect living things and communities.

floodplain: the area of land beside a river or stream that is covered with water during a flood.

heritage: traditions and objects of value passed down through several generations.

ice age: a period of time when the earth is very cold and lots of water in the oceans turns to ice.

intermarriage: a term used to describe marriages between members of different groups.

Iroquoian: describes a large family of Indian languages, mostly in eastern North America, which includes those of the Cherokees and Mohawks.

irrigation: any system for watering the land to grow plants.

medicine man: a religious leader and healer.

migration: movement from one place to another.

minority: the smaller in number of two groups forming a whole.

missionaries: people who try to teach others their religion.

moccasins: soft shoes made of a single piece of leather.

myth: a traditional story that explains beliefs or events in nature.

nation: people who have their own customs, laws, and land separate from other nations or people.

persecution: treating someone or a certain group of people badly over a period of time.

playwright: a person who writes plays.

prejudice: dislike or injustice that is not based on reason or experience.

refugee: a person who is forced to leave his or her home to find safety and protection.

reservation: land set aside by the U.S. government.

stockades: large prison camps surrounded by fences and guarded by soldiers.

treaty: an agreement among nations or people.

MORE RESOURCES

Websites:

http://www.bigorrin.org/cherokee_kids.htm
Facts about the Cherokees for children.

http://www.cherokee.org
The official website of the Cherokee Nation.

http://www.cherokee.org/Extras/Downloads/syllabary.html
Sound files of Cherokee syllabary.

http://cherokeeartistsassociation.org/
A website promoting individual Cherokee artists and craftspeople.

http://www.cherokeebyblood.com/
Covers many topics such as medicine, cookery, religion, housing, clothing, hunting, and weapons.

http://www.cherokeeheritage.org/
A website by and about the Cherokee Heritage Center in Tahlequah, Oklahoma.

http://www.cherokeemuseum.org/
A website by and about the Museum of the Cherokee Indian in Cherokee, North Carolina.

http://www.cherokeephoenix.org/default.aspx
News from the *Cherokee Phoenix*.

http://www.native-languages.org/cherokee_alphabet.htm
Information about the Cherokee syllabary, how to pronounce it, and some Cherokee words for animals, colors, and body parts.

http://www.sacred-texts.com/nam/cher/motc/index.htm
More than one hundred Cherokee myths published in 1898.

http://www.sequoyahmuseum.org
The website of the Sequoyah Birthplace Museum in Vonore, Tennessee.

http://www.unitedkeetoowahband.org/
The official website of the United Keetoowah Band of Cherokee Indians.

DVDs:

We Shall Remain. PBS, 2009.

500 Nations. Warner Home Video, 2004.

Books:

Aller, Susan Bivin. *Why Did Cherokees Move West? And Other Questions About the Trail of Tears (Six Questions of American History).* Lerner Publications, 2010.

Basel, Roberta. *Sequoyah: Inventor of Written Cherokee (Signature Lives).* Compass Point Books, 2008.

Dell, Pamela. *Wilma Mankiller: Chief of the Cherokee Nation (Signature Lives).* Compass Point Books, 2005.

Donlan, Leni. *Cherokee Rose (American History Through Primary Sources).* Raintree, 2007.

Duncan, Barbara R., ed. *The Origin of the Milky Way: And Other Living Stories of the Cherokee.* University of North Carolina Press, 2010.

Englar, Mary. *The Cherokee and Their History (We the People).* Compass Point Books, 2005.

Fradin, Dennis B. *The Trail of Tears (Turning Points of U.S. History).* Benchmark Books, 2007.

Gibson, Karen Bush. *Native American History for Kids: With 21 Activities.* Chicago Review Press, 2010.

Hook, Sue Vander. *Trail of Tears (Essential Events).* ABDO Publishing Company, 2010.

Johnson, Michael. *Native Tribes of the Southeast (Native Tribes of North America).* World Almanac Library, 2004.

Kent, Deborah. *The Trail of Tears (Cornerstones of Freedom).* Children's Press, 2007.

Murdoch, David S. *North American Indian (DK Eyewitness Books).* DK Children, 2005.

Tapper, Suzanne Cloud. *The Cherokee: A Proud People (American Indians).* Enslow Elementary, 2005.

Wade, Mary Dodson. *Amazing Cherokee Writer Sequoyah (Amazing Americans).* Enslow Elementary, 2009.

THINGS TO THINK ABOUT AND DO

YOU ARE THERE

Pretend you are a newspaper reporter in 1838. Write a short newspaper article about General Winfield Scott's U.S. Army troops taking the Cherokees from their homes and putting them in stockades.

NEGOTIATING A TREATY

Imagine that you are one of the Cherokees negotiating the treaty of 1835 that includes the United States' desire to move the Cherokees to Indian Territory (now Oklahoma). Make a list of the arguments you might make for allowing the Cherokees to remain in their homeland in the East.

STARTING OVER

Imagine that your Cherokee family has just arrived in the wilderness in the West at the end of the Trail of Tears. Write a short essay about all that would have to be done to start life over in that new place.

SETTING THE SCENE

Draw a picture of a Cherokee town complete with homes and farms. Include people in traditional clothing.

A TERRIBLE JOURNEY

Imagine yourself a young Cherokee forced to leave your homeland, and write a day-by-day diary of the Trail of Tears.

INDEX

Adena culture 6
Alaska 4
American Indian Movement 9
Appalachian Mountains 4, 6, 7, 10, 11
arts 31, 32
Asia 4–5

beadwork 31
beliefs 8, 14, 28
Bering Strait 4
Berry, Martha 31
blowguns 34
Booger Dance 28
Burnett, John G. 16

Cahokia 6
Canada 4, 10
Cherokee Heritage Center 9, 22, 23, 38
Cherokee Nation 10, 15, 18, 19, 34–35, 36, 37
Cherokee National Supreme Court Museum 39
Cherokee National Youth Choir 39
Cherokee, North Carolina 38
Cherokee syllabary 7, 14, 39
Chickasaws 21
children 22–23, 29, 33
Choctaws 21
Civil War 18–19

clothes 23
Conley, Robert J. 31
Creeks 21

dancing 28, 29
diseases 6, 18
Duvall, Deborah L. 32

Eastern Cherokees 10, 11, 16–17, 33–34
education 8, 14, 18, 36, 38, 39
employment 33, 35
Europeans 6, 12–13

family life 22–23
farming 5, 12, 20, 34
fishing 5, 20
Five Civilized Tribes 21
food 20

games 24–25, 26–27, 34
gathering food 5, 12, 21
gold rush 14, 15
government 14, 18, 22, 35
Great Smoky Mountains National Park 11, 33
guns 6, 7

Hobson, Geary 30
Hopewell culture 6
horses 6, 7
housing 5, 22

hunting 5, 12, 20, 21, 23

Indian Removal Act 15

Jackson, Andrew 15
Jacob, Murv 32
Jefferson, Thomas 13

Kituwah Language Academy 38

language 7, 8, 14, 38, 39
laws 14, 39
Lindneux, Robert 17
literature 30, 31, 32
Louisiana Purchase 13

Mankiller, Wilma 37
McAlister, Barbara 31
medicine 24
migrations 4–5, 8, 11, 16–17
missionaries 14
movies 31
Muscogees 21
Museum of the Cherokee Indian 38
myths and stories 10–11, 24, 26–27

newspapers 14, 18, 39

Oklahoma 8
origins 10–11

politics 8, 9
pottery 21

Qualla Boundary reservation 10, 33

reservations 8, 9
Riggs, Lynn 30
Rogers, Will 30
Ross, Gail 31
Ross, John, Chief 15, 17

Scott, Winfield 16
Secotan, North Carolina 12
Seminoles 21
Sequoyah 7, 14
Sequoyah High School 36
singing 39
Society of American Indians 8
Stanley, John Mix 18
stickball 24–25
Stomp Dance 29
Strickland, Rennard 30
Studi, Wes 31

Tahlequah, Oklahoma 18, 34–35, 36, 37, 38, 39
Thomas, William 33
trade 6, 12, 13, 21
Trail of Tears 16, 17

United Keetoowah Band of Cherokee Indians 34

villages and towns 6, 9, 12, 22

war 12–13, 23